unbroken

Bob MacKenzie

O the land of cloudless day,
O the land of an unclouded day,
O they tell me of a home where no storm clouds rise,
O they tell me of an unclouded day.

J. K. Alwood, 1879

Other Books by Bob MacKenzie

Poetry

footsteps in the garden, Cyberwit.com, 2021
somewhere still in wind the tree is bending, Silver Bow, 2018
Agapé: Heaven & Earth, Dark Matter Press, 2015
Spirit Quest (with Sharlena Wood, artist), Dark Matter Press, 2014
On Edge, Dark Matter Press, 2012
Songrise, Dark Matter Press, 2012
Innocent (I wasn't there), Thee Hellbox Press, 2008
Audio-Visuals, Sarnia Public Art Gallery, 1973
Reflection, self-published, 1966

Prose Fiction

The Hired Gun (Mike St. Pierre, illust.), Dark Matter Press, 2016
Another Eternity, Dark Matter Press, 2012
A Gathering of Shadows, Dark Matter Press, 2012
Ghost Shadow: Unfinished Sins, Dark Matter Press, 2010
To Whom It May Concern, Dark Matter Press, 2010
A Beautiful Day to Be Dead (collab.), Thee Hellbox Press, 2008
To Whom It May Concern (e-book), Amazon Shorts, 2006
Ghost Shadow: Unfinished Sins (hypertext), Poet Pourri, 1999
The Little Song, Brandstead Press, 1975

unbroken
Bob MacKenzie

Acknowledgements

The cover photograph is by Engin Akyurt.
https://www.pexels.com/photo/silhouette-photo-of-woman-
1446948

"After the Dark" was first published in Lothlorien Poetry Journal,
Volume 8, Thursday, March 3, 2022.
https://lothlorienpoetryjournal.blogspot.com/2022/03/five-poems-
by-bob-mackenzie.html

Table of Contents

outliers

it was 1961 in a small prairie town
and the Fifties were still hanging on
held back by the dirt farmer culture
born long ago and not ready to change
a town of dirt streets and pickup trucks
of small shops and unbending beliefs
a world firmly grounded in the past
until summer brought the outsiders

the lake was popular with tourists all summer
once known as Snake Lake now Sylvan Lake
nine miles long but not wide I recall
shallow at the shore and quite far out
and a long sand beach at the south end
between the downtown and the water
thick weeds in the water near the shore
where leeches wait to dine on boys' blood

population got ten times bigger each summer
when outsiders filled the streets and beach
and Lakeshore Drive became a fairground
midway rides and hucksters on each corner
crowds big enough for a boy to hide
unseen for just a while and feel safe
an outsider among outsiders
streets alive with carnival magic

after grade seven my family moved again
always the new kid always alone
it was time once more to make new friends
hard in a school from grades eight to twelve
kids brought by bus from towns near and far
that first summer surreal on Lakeshore
serene in the sunshine on the beach
this boy not sure it's dream or nightmare

starting over again in Sylvan Lake was hard
in grade eight I didn't make close friends
hung out with kids my age at lunch break
shared some time but were gone at day's end
this school put me in the youngest group
down from middle grade in junior high
and older bullies sought easy prey
like me as a new boy and Ricky.

Ricky wanted to be a rock and roll hero
I just longed to fit in if I could
Ricky dressed in the rock and roll style
long blond hair teased into a ducktail
clothes the essence of Gene Vincent cool
standing in the shadows I stood out
always the outsider looking in
the new kid who never felt welcome

I'm not sure how Ricky and I had met that fall
but we saw something in each other
shared deep inside and became best friends
he the flash and me there in the shadows
perfect prey for the highschool bullies
and the beatings that were sure to come
after school and even on weekends
whenever they tracked one of us down

during the winter Ricky and me turned fourteen
little changed but a new year began
without promise and cold as before
school closed for a week in December
after the well froze in a cold snap
then nothing much happened until spring
and Ricky and me breathed easier
though we knew the bullies were waiting

it was 1961 in this small minded town
and the Fifties were still hanging on
held back by the dirt farmer culture
born long ago and not ready to change
a town of dirt streets and pickup trucks
of small shops and unbending beliefs
a world firmly grounded in the past
and Ricky and me were not welcome

it was never one bully but a gang of toughs
caught up and circled me after school
one against one was thought a fair fight
except one was seventeen years old
the other just a boy of fourteen
and when the bully tired he stepped out
made way for another to step in
keep on fighting the boy one-on-one

there'd be no such one-on-one fair fight for Ricky
if the bullies saw me as weak prey
Ricky was someone perfect to hate
too pretty in his rock and roll way
a fairy like their dads would beat up
on a Saturday night drunken whim
homo queer they called him all the names
beat him up though he was none of those

who said this is the winter of our discontent
got our world just right that cold winter
fourteen years old and living in fear
drawn to each other by circumstance
bullied and beaten by too many
not able to fit in with the rest
our own small society of two
just boys and ever so alone

it was spring when the boys caught me in the schoolyard
caught me unawares in the lunch break
circled round while one pushed and hit me
egged on by others in the circle
nothing for me to do but fight back
he didn't hear the circle's shouted tips
I heard them and beat him to the ground
teachers stopped me or I'd have killed him

Later that spring Ricky was found dead in the woods
his killers never brought to justice
police work short and sweet and case closed
who killed him was not a mystery
Ricky had been tracked and beat to death
and I could do nothing about it
a fourteen year old boy on his own
haunted by a circle of bullies

it was 1961 in a small-minded town
and the Fifties were still hanging on
held back by its dirt farmer culture
born long ago and not ready to change
a town of dirt streets and pickup trucks
of small shops and unbending beliefs
a world firmly grounded in the past
where evil waits to dine on boys' blood

in the summer my family moved again
it was time once more to make new friends
always the new kid always alone
just wanting to fit in if I can
and with a new school came new dangers
but I had changed and can not forget
my friend found and lost in a moment
who could have been a rock and roll star

perdition

55

I've seen this image many times before
paintings, photographs, the same noir film scenes
always the same man in the same city

office towers become menacing forms
loom over desolate streets of shadows
perhaps a gauntlet for the unwary

silhouette of fedora and trenchcoat
a man walks away toward the distant
afterglow separating dusk from dark

I wake suddenly startled by sunlight
slumped near a dumpster in some alley
my coat like a blanket wrapped around me

in my hand there's an empty wine bottle
there's nothing around me but scattered trash
none of this alleyway scene is my life

12

Ireland remains a distant misty dream
land of faerie magic told as legend
echoed in the songs sung by Ma and Pa

we left Ireland before I could know it
fled New York in a rush to Alberta
lived the life of wild rovers on the run

my pa may have been a Provisional
involved too deep in the revolution
but I never knew just what he had done

my sister was born dead when I was twelve
the year I learned of personal sorrow
soul deep and eternal for Ma and Pa

some men came to town asking after Pa
Mounties or British agents Pa had guessed
time had come for us to move once again

my pa drove up as I walked home from school
"we're moving now" he said "get in the car"
one more secret move before morning came

15

it's not a real city as was New York
where Pa could hide among other Irish
yet here in Calgary a man can thrive

in a country where gambling's illegal
the cops leave the Irish Sweepstakes alone
not a real secret when everyone plays

out in the open where all play the sweeps
Pa supplies dealers bulk tickets to sell
rakes in as much as numbers in New York

I pick up crates of sweepstake ticket books
shipped out from Ireland to Montreal
labelled "table jellies" for the customs

cops and customs agents paid and blind-eyed
crates come to Calgary still not opened
tickets ready to sell sweepstakes dreamers

as Pa's number-two I'm doing alright
just below the radar where life is good
British agents and Mounties out of mind

our networks are efficient and tempting
cartels and syndicates reach out to us
not criminals like they are we resist

17

with money and power and threats implied
out of town mobsters tried to seduce us
nearly two years now and we are still here

mobsters and bikers were here before us
low level conmen and fast-buckaneers
unsafe bad actors who we'd never hire

big-time crime has come since to Calgary
with its heavy drugs and gangland murders
corrupt police and politics the norm

the Irish gangs have stayed in big cities
know that we're here but leave us alone
keep watch in case they need to protect us

we can't avoid contact with organized crime
nobody's not touched by their presence here now
but I've kept us straight and expanded our firm

sweepstakes earnings build up our interests
loans and financing buy us companies
car lots and shops and professional firms

our new public face has brought us respect
from workers up to the mayor himself
cops tip their hats and bosses ask advice

21

we walked out of Hy's Steakhouse on Friday
the street was empty then the car flew by
I pushed Ma to the ground as bullets flew

bullets found Pa and he fell to the ground
dead by morning in a hospital bed
the bastards killed Pa and right must be done

he's just a hooligan come off the street
is young Jimmy Sills yet still he must die
as must the boy who had driven the car

this murder had not come here from Ireland
our past well hidden this hit was local
one of the big mobs did this and must pay

Jimmy talked and told all before he died
gave up the driver and who called the hit
Yank mob boss Lou Logan had broken the peace

Lou's bosses want peace as much as we do
shot him down on the street to warn others
justice is done and our balance restored

the cathedral full and Pa's cortege long
respect was paid by poor to powerful
next day I became top man in our firm

28

a lot has changed since the day we lost Pa
since I became head of our family firm
nothing is certain as the world we knew

the syndicates and mobs grow here like weeds
godfathers and gangsters and organized crime
our cowtown become the home to mean streets

Patrick Brennan lies dead now in his grave
unknown as Sean Flannery sought by the Brits
still we stay under the radar where safe

gone seven years since Pa was murdered
I still run the firm as he'd have wanted
never cross the line that he drew for us

legal gambling has swallowed the sweepstakes
underground gambling's run by the gangsters
there's no percentage for us in this now

we stay legit and keep the cops friendly
keep some things quiet and always low key
perhaps not straight but never over the line

the future looks bright for this wild rover
the firm is doing well and growing fast
and I'll marry my Mary in the spring

36

seven years we've been wed Mary and me
Seamus is seven and Fiona five
another on the way may be the last

fate's been kind to us and good to Brennan's
the firm's doing well and mostly legit
what's not is well hidden from prying eyes

Ma is now set in a place of her own
comes to see us and spoil Seamus and Fi
it's good to see her share the children's joy

peace has come to this family at last
far from the troubles we fled for so long
Ireland a dream now we've left far behind

44

the big crews are pros shy of exposure
we Brennans also stay out of the light
now outsider cowboys put all at risk

new players in town take on all comers
have started a shooting war in earnest
all we have is up for grabs in this war

the war is on and there's blood in the streets
victims dead from street soldiers to bosses
gunned down in drive-bys or just disappeared

after thirty years our firm's in trouble
targetted by police and gangsters both
respect and trust no longer protect us

I fear I'm losing all I have gained
I drink too much according to Mary
no longer the man that she had married

the firm is closing and Mary leaving
divorce and bankruptcy are all I face
the end is coming and I need a drink

55

Seamus and Fi visit me in my room
Mary sends greetings but she stays away
the doctors say I had a heart attack

Seamus tells me I was found on the street
slumped against a dumpster at a lane's end
good as dead I was and now I lie here

how has my life come to be only this
a bit of trash found left in an alley
laid in a bed in a hospital room

in the quiet of night peace comes easy
footsteps pass softly by in the hallway
I am left alone with my memories

come night I lie back and I close my eyes
walk among shadows along a dark street
ahead of me see the distant light burn

the street is starting to fill up with mist
pleasant and warm and I follow the light
where a door is open and I pass through

After the Dark

They are wrong, you know, about the dark;
before the dawn it is much diminished
and is flecked with light in particles
large enough to make a difference. Dawn
by then has sent its spores to plant them
selves in us and erode the darker self
we carry, each of us, deep within.

Oh no, the dark when it is darkest comes
after dusk. The sun casts a dark shade
behind itself, dusk the edge of blackest
night which follows the sun's light passing
too soon over us so that we must all
feel the chill of dark in some degree.

This is the dark into which I was born
long ago, that night of wind and sleet
howling round and through that mountain cabin,
and this is the dark within me still
as I approach that greater dark abyss
into which we all must fall at last.

It is into this dark he too was born,
far from here and far from now, of light
and fire in a valley far from his kind.
But I leap ahead of my story!
It all begins long before that secret birth,
before his birth and before mine.

Long ago and far away, the old stories
begin: yet was this so long ago
and what place in those times was so far off?
No, I might say it all began here,
and those days not so long ago at all.

They say that men were gods. Light and fire
playthings, and the very winds like highways
upon which men would fly. They say these
and other things which the people believe,
but I am of another time, dark
and unbelieving without my seeing
with my own eyes proof of these wonders.

I will say only that there are legends,
and that somewhere in these ancient tales
may lay the truth of the matter. Just that,
plus that I have been to the plains once,
in my youth, have seen great cities empty
and in ruin. How they were built, by whom,
and how destroyed, I would not guess.

I know only that they exist, that legends
tell of a race of giants, powerful
enough to conquer the universe,
a race that had harnessed all the magic,
and made it serve the needs of men, fire
and light and all the great forces, perhaps
even that great force that rules all others.

Such a race could raise cities on the plains
as I have seen, and ruin them, but
if the legends are true I do not know,
or if there is some other answer.
That is for wiser minds than mine to tell.

I shall tell of a later time, then,
after the time of which the legends speak:
shall tell of a time of deepest dark
in every soul throughout the land. This
is the time when he was born, and I,
who became his friend: shadow to his light.

Yet, if you would understand my tale,
I must tell something of that other time:
both of the legends and of the truth,
for it is from this my story begins.

Long before the time of darkness came,
there was more than this we call The People,
than these hills and valleys we live in,
than the plains below where no one dares go.
It is said the land stretches far beyond
the edge of reality, and beyond
waters even wider reach worlds
as great as this. Even the sky, it is said,
was blue as a mountain lake is green,
and broad as the waters at the land's end,
and beyond it too were other worlds.

Man, the legends say, ruled over all this;
then were the days long and nights made light;
Man travelled the universe end to end,
his wondrous vehicles drawn by powers
taken from the gods themselves. From the gods
Man took fire and light; from the gods too
Man took the power to move through the sky
and across the great seas of water
and across the vast lands at great speed.

Gods men came finally to consider
themselves: of great cities and great tribes, both
builders and destroyers. Man's power,
taken from the gods, became all power,
ruled the universe, answerable
to no man or god, growing beyond man,
itself finally ruling, power
taken from the god's control, never in
Man's control.

The fires when they came, came
from the dark and with the dark, filling all
the universe with darkness no man
escapes for long. The legends do not tell
how some men lived, made shelters high up
in these hills, how then their children's children
made their way to the valleys after,
becoming in time the tribes of the land,
the tribes who to this day rule the land.

None of this is known, for this was the time
darkness filled the land. This was the dark
he came into so long ago, bringing light,
although we could not have known back then
he was the one of whom the legends spoke.

There's Something About Persephone

For me, it is always darkest winter,
and even that part of me who can live
outside always feels the cold reach upward
to pull me back and down into that dark
palace where I hide: I, Persephone,
waiting for some spring to come to darkness,
fearing dark Hades instead will find me.

> *I might have been thirteen when I first heard the*
> *myth, told me by Mom perhaps or read in a book.*
> *For some reason it drew me in, this tale of a girl*
> *taken by a bad man into his palace underground*
> *and her mother unable to stop it. How her mother*
> *managed to save this girl for half the year and made*
> *the difference between winter and spring. Now I am*
> *twenty and I live this story in my dreams.*

I am Spring, named in a time when fashion
named children after flowers and seasons,
named for a time of rebirth and new life,
named by Hades, who desolates all light
and beauty and called himself my father,
called himself Love in the light but grew dark
with the lust to destroy all spring, all life.

> *Mommy and Daddy were hippies I suppose, though*
> *we never lived in a commune or anything like that.*
> *Daddy was a musician part-time when he wasn't on*
> *the job in construction and Mommy kept house and*
> *taught me to paint. I remember sunny days and fun*
> *in the park, but don't remember nights at all, until I*
> *dream that is.*

Before memory, my father was all–
to me tall and handsome and wise and kind–
all Persephone must have thought Hades
as he walked out across the sunlit fields
and smiled at her and invited her home
somewhere down the river: a dark palace
he described as glittering and vibrant.

> *I imagine Persephone and Demeter her mother in*
> *those green fields filled with sunshine and flowers,*
> *invited by a prince back to his palace. I wonder if it*
> *all had seemed wonderful or if his intentions were*
> *clear all the time. The story goes that Demeter*
> *cautioned her daughter but still let her go down to*
> *the palace.*

That long ago Persephone escaped
with half her life locked in Hades' palace
but half again filled with sun and flowers;
my Persephone hides in a dark room
deep below the palace and cannot leave,
and even Spring, who waits outside, always
walks in darkness and deathly cold for her.

> *A deep chill comes over me sometimes for no*
> *reason. Like a ghost had touched me, and I'm*
> *suddenly afraid though I don't know why.*

I had forgotten most of my lifetime.
Spring lived on eternal in the present,
needing no past life and planning no future,
and Persephone was well and truly
buried; Spring lived on, but heard the voices,
past lives whispering their dark vaulted words:
remember your sister deep in the palace.

*For a very long time I felt there was something I
needed to remember, to tell. I never knew what.
Whatever it was, it scared me and I was unable to
go there. Sudden glimpses were quickly squelched
when I was awake, and nightmares blocked out by
morning light. I knew there was something I should
remember but would not allow in the light.*

I am Spring, I cried, I have no sister,
no Persephone, hid in some dark room.
I am Spring, I cried, and I knew I lied
to hide something and had no idea
what dark secret lay below the palace
protected by my long forgetfulness,
protecting, as much as anything, me.

*The shadows scare me, the ones you see just out of
the corner of your eye, and sometimes sounds too
for a moment. It's like they bring a sudden dark
memory, so quick I feel it but don't really remember
after all.*

Spring remembered my father in a time
he loved my mother and he loved me too;
he was Daddy, my protector, my God.
In the memory, I am a young girl,
seven at most; Spring has no memory
after that until I am a grown woman.
Persephone remembers all of it.

*I remember the trips we took to the park and to the
zoo and birthday parties and the fun we had when
Daddy was around. I was Daddy's little girl and I
knew he loved me. So now that I'm older why do I
feel something's not right? Sudden memories in the
daytime scare me. And the dreams are the worst.*

Persephone in the dark in her cell
remembers all of it and wants to tell
if only Spring will batter down the walls
and release her into the white sunshine
she recalls so well from ancient times
when Daddy was a God Persephone
could trust to guard her from all the darkness.

> *Even with best friends I can't let down my guard. If
> I'm not watchful I slip and see, what? It's like
> there's something dark and evil trying to get out and
> I've got to keep it in. Yet I don't know what it is I'm
> afraid of.*

It was she who came to me in my dreams:
Persephone from that dark underworld
where for thirty years I had hidden her,
thought her dead and gone and all memory
taken with her into some deep black hole
far beneath the palace, where I was safe,
where Spring was safe from forgotten terror.

> *I wake in the dark shaking, but I can't shake these
> dreams when they come. Afterward sleep doesn't
> come easy.*

In my dreams, I became Persephone,
lost to me for all those forgotten years,
and Spring became like a dream hovering
out of my reach but close enough that now
my hope for Spring was my greatest torture,
my fear for Spring's agony greater than
any terror Persephone might endure.

*I don't understand. I've had a happy childhood and
teen years and I'm happy now. I really am. So why
have I started having night terrors that feel like
flashbacks and sudden flashes in daytime? It just
doesn't make sense.*

I am Spring, born in the sunshine to live
seven glowing years, then asleep thirty
before waking in dust, in grey ashes
from which I rise in agony and seek life
for me and for Persephone below.
Thirty years have I walked among the dead
and been one of them; now I live again.

*Trust is an issue. I'm uncomfortable with men and I
don't know why. I just don't trust any man. In fact,
I'm afraid of most men. And I'm wary with women.
I never know when one might betray me, yet I see no
reason they would. It's hard for me to let anyone in.
I just don't.*

There was a body Spring that walked the earth,
had friends, had men, was seen by all to live
and prosper–destitute and void inside.
Spring never let the friends inside the wall
she had built with such care; she used the men
for physical comfort, all without love.
Spring had men; Persephone never did.

*That Demeter! What was she thinking, letting her
daughter go off alone with that man? Why didn't
she stop him? Or at least insist on going along?
She was the mom, should have stood up for
Persephone. She must have known what Hades was
really after. Some nights I am Persephone in my
dreams.*

Persephone persisted deep inside
that black hole watching Spring, the waking dead,
doing what others expected of her,
touched by nothing: void inside, void outside.
Persephone, alone and forgotten,
longed for release, for freedom, for sunshine,
for the life she knew she could give to Spring.

> *Some nights, too many nights, it's hard for me to
> sleep. More than the dark of night, I fear the dark
> hole I sense inside me. What if I fall in and can't
> ever get back out?*

Persephone was there when Spring awoke,
her hand rising out of the dark ashes
to take Spring's and guide her out of the dark.
Spring ran screaming through the darkness, away
from that apparition, from that dark hand
reaching out from the dark cell she had built
in pain so long ago and thought was safe.

> *There's something I should remember but can't. I
> wonder which I fear most, to never remember or to
> remember it all at last.*

They named me Spring Sunshine more for fashion
than anything else and called me Spring without
Sunshine forever after; I am Spring,
dark and without soul, lost in dust and ash.
I knew Daddy died when I was seven,
and the other took his body and soul,
and the other in him took Spring for himself.

*He creeps into my room in dreams not long after
Mom falls asleep. Gently slips the covers off me.
Whispers everything is alright as he lies down
beside me. I can't see who he is, can't remember.
The dream becomes a blur. I am naked and he is
touching me, kissing me. As the dream fades to
black all I hear is everything is alright. I know I
mustn't tell.*

Persephone ran into the darkness,
away from that greater dark inside him,
ran deep into the palace, where she hid,
locked in a dark and windowless closet
Spring had built for her; Persephone ran,
and Spring lay down in the ashes and died
just as her Daddy had–but lived within.

*The dream is too real. Oh God! I don't know who
the man is who comes to my bed, but I wish he was
dead, I wish I was dead.*

Spring was thirty-five when he died again.
They told her he was dead; she knew better.
She knew Daddy's soul was lost long ago,
and now the body was gone, but she knew
that dark thing inside him would never die,
and she began to be afraid again.
Within two years, dark dreams came to find Spring.

*Night terrors are worse now. I wake in a sweat
afraid to go back to sleep. I wish I knew what's
happening to me. There are times I can't breathe
when something, almost anything I think, triggers
the daytime flashes ever more vivid.*

As far as she could see, grey ash spread out
across a broad, even plain to the sky,
a sky so grey there was no horizon,
so that Spring's world was without form and void.
Near her side the grey ash moved and took shape
as she watched fascinated; a grey hand
rose from below, reaching for her own hand.

> *All I want to do is run away. How do you run away*
> *from a dream? He comes to me every night now,*
> *too real to be only a dream. Am I going crazy?*
> *Nothing seems real anymore, yet all too real.*

Spring fled into the ashen haze spun up
by her own flying feet until she vanished
and even she was without form and quite void
in this grey world bereft of memory.
Somewhere far away, she could sense an arm
sinking slowly through grey ash to some black
hole below, and she wondered how she knew.

> *I can't tell anyone. Can't talk about this man who*
> *comes to me in dreams. Who will believe me?*
> *Everything is alright has become my new mantra.*
> *I'm fine I say when they ask. All I want to do is run*
> *away.*

Spring ran and ran through the grey, not seeing
the grey run into black, bind her in black.
Persephone felt the rope chafe her wrist
as her sister hung in some dark closet
and knew who had done this; Spring saw dark shapes,
nothing more–but she knew some dark evil
had come back for her, and she knew terror.

He is not just touching me. I'm trapped and he's on top of me, pushing. Oh, it hurts! And I can't move, can't do anything to stop him. He is inside me, inside my darkest dreams. When he's done he whispers everything is alright and fades into the night like a ghost. And I know I mustn't tell.

Hanging in the closet by her wrists, Spring
sensed the dark being who had hung her there,
but could also feel that grey arm and hand
reaching out to her; somehow she drew hope
and knew the owner of that arm would help.
The rope cut into her wrist and she prayed
the darkness would go away forever.

I wish I was dead.

Out of the grey plain the darkness came down,
falling on Spring with something long and lithe:
skipping rope, or belt, or serpent of fire
burning fiercely as it whipped into her flesh.
The sound came, at first distant, but growing
to fill the vast plain, to wrap and fill Spring;
Persephone knew the sound was her screams.

I open my mouth but I can't scream. I can't breathe. He comes to me every night now. Touches me all over. Has his pleasure then leaves. Everything is alright. I wake but remember the dream. Everything is not alright. I cry myself back to sleep.

Once, the grey hand brushed against hers briefly,
then was gone, but it gave Spring brief solace,
and she understood her sister was near.
So was the faceless form that tied her up,
beat her, raped her, battered her, made her fear
her life would end; each time she dreamed, she saw
the face becoming clearer, and she knew him.

> *I see his face, almost. No! I don't want to know
> this. I do not want to know. Then he's on top of me
> again, inside me again and I can do nothing to stop
> him. I wish he was dead. I wish these dreams would
> just stop.*

Spring knew the face forming from the blackness,
but she could not quite make out who it was;
Persephone knew, but she could not tell,
not name the evil that Spring saw in dreams.
The dreams changed only a little, but grew,
so the plain took on form as the face formed
on the blackness, and Spring formed memories.

> *I see bits of the face like it's fading into view. But
> not clear, not clear. Like a ghost of someone I
> knew. I don't want to know who he is, this man who
> comes to me each night. Yet somewhere in the back
> of my mind I remember.*

The sun warmed Persephone as the man
smiled at her and held out his hand warmly.
Come in here, he said, and see my palace;
I'll show you a world you'll never forget.
Hades crossed the meadow into darkness;
as he walked into the dark pit, she called,
Daddy, wait for me–and the dark took her.

No! I don't want to know. Don't want to
remember. Daddy comes to kiss me good night.
That is all. Daddy just comes to kiss me good night.
And I am crying.

The rape came to Spring softly, like a scene
in a play, done and done again to her
or someone else; she was never certain.
Was it Persephone bathed in blood red
light on the stage, and Spring watching the show?
Or did all the black of night cover Spring
as Persephone sadly watched her die?

It all seems unreal now, like the girl is not me lying
there in her bed. Afraid and waiting. She knows he
will come. She knows he will have her again. And
she can do nothing to stop him. She mustn't tell.
Everything is alright.

Without mercy, someone had been beaten;
someone had been bound, tied for days and left,
hung in a closet, hid in a basement,
always with the door shut and no windows,
hung in the dark; someone had been tortured,
torn apart by some dark and monstrous being.
Spring wondered, had it been Persephone?

Am I going crazy? I feel like I'm being torn apart,
like there's another girl inside me who has been
hurt so bad. And I see but can't help her. Can't
help me. Can't tell anyone. I just wish it would
end. If anyone asks, I'm fine.

Once, when Hades briefly stopped watching her,
someone took Persephone by the hand,
led her deep into the palace, deep below
where Hades never went–a secret room.
Here you'll be safe, the other girl told her,
then began to brick up the door with black bricks.
Dark sorrow closed in on Persephone.

> *I feel like walls are crashing down. Like demons*
> *are being released I may not want to meet. I am*
> *constantly afraid. To sleep perchance to dream as*
> *the poet wrote. My dreams are worse than death. I*
> *see that face ever more clearly now in my dreams.*
> *I'd rather die than know.*

With Persephone safe, though forever
trapped deep in Hades' palace, Spring escaped,
but found no sunny meadow waiting her.
As far as she could see, grey ash spread out
across a broad, even plain to the sky,
a sky so grey there was no horizon,
so that Spring's world was without form and void.

> *I'm lost. Nothing interests me anymore. The*
> *terrors have taken over and I live in dark dreams.*
> *The man comes to me and whispers his love.*
> *Touches me and rapes me and I can do nothing.*
> *Everything is not alright. I'm fine I say. I'm fine.*

Like whirling dust devils from her childhood,
whirlwinds rose from the ash and formed themselves,
subtly becoming forms of a gone world
Spring might once have lived in, stripped to reveal
all the outrage and terror just below,
in that dark palace; only Persephone–
only she–knew there was no room for Spring.

*I'm angry all the time. I rage at my friends and
don't know why. I have outbursts at family and
strangers. I can't sleep and I don't eat. What's
wrong with me? What's wrong? Nothing is alright.
I'm not fine.*

In the grey before dawn, her room was plain,
forcing its form out of the fading night
as she sat up in her bed, not yet sure
the still black corners did not hide lithe forms
waiting the right moment to pounce on her,
to tear her from her bed, back to darkness
Hades had led her into long ago.

*I'm angry. And I'm terribly afraid. I mustn't tell.
Not anyone. Not even. Not even me.*

Persephone cowered in her black room,
hid in a corner, tried not to be seen.
She had heard that great door of stone open,
heard the darkness come to life with demons
set free, heard them rushing from the palace
into Spring's world, and heard them rushing down
some dark stairs toward her, Persephone.

*The dark is rushing in on me. Can't sleep for fear
the man will come, will take me again. My dreams
have become so real they feel like memories.
Memories I don't want to have. Is this how the girl
Persephone must have felt down in Hades' palace?
Why didn't Mommy protect me?*

Spring sat up in her bed, watching shadows
from the darkest corners, grey mists dancing,
dervish forms slipping out of the darkness
to grasp her and hold her pinned to the bed.
As he had so long ago, he came now
from the blackest corner of eternity.
Hades came again to Spring and took her.

> *The man quietly creeps into my room and into my*
> *dreams. He makes me quiver. He makes me cry.*
> *He makes me his and I am very afraid. Every night*
> *he comes to my bed and he takes me. Everything is*
> *alright he says.*

Spring knew the face that formed from the blackness,
knew it was Hades, knew he was changing,
putting on the mask, forming the face she knew.
The face became clear as Hades took her,
covering her in all blackness and death;
in that brief moment, the face became clear.
Hades took Spring by force; Spring saw his face.

> *I can almost see it now. The man's face forming in*
> *the darkness. Becoming real in my dream. I close*
> *my eyes. I do not want to know. Something is not*
> *alright. Something is very wrong.*

Persephone screamed as the wall crashed in,
then fled the blackness pursuing her,
fled her small black cell, fled that black palace,
and ran up and up along the river
seeking spring sunshine above the grey ash.
Persephone felt the pain and knew Spring,
her sister, had seen the face of evil.

I close my eyes. The man who comes to my bed in dreams cannot have this face. I will not see it. I will not. What the hell was Demeter thinking, letting this man take her daughter? What was Mommy thinking?

Spring fought, but there was no escape for her.
The darkness held her arms and legs tightly
and Hades came and smothered her in black
death that took her as it had long ago.
Spring died the death of the living, buried
herself deep in her heart, leaving nothing
for him; no, she cried, no Daddy, don't!

I've seen his face. Nothing is alright. I remember now. He came to my bed night after night. Kissed me as he pulled my covers off. Everything's alright he said. Got in bed beside me. Touched me. Got on top. Raped me. How could he do that? Tears are not enough. I mustn't tell. I'm fine I say.

The grey hand rose from the ash grey of dawn
and reached for Spring somewhere in the darkness;
Persephone rose from the sea of ash
slowly, wary of the darkness waiting
to take her as her sister was taken.
She rose until she could see that evil
Hades taking her dying sister, Spring.

The legend is wrong. Demeter made a deal with Hades to free Persephone. Something about a partly eaten pomegranate. For this she is praised. But this mother only got back half her daughter's life. Never the half still hid beneath the surface. Persephone is not fine. I am not fine.

The grey hand rose from the ash grey of dawn;
grey as her hand, the woman from the ash
stood naked before Spring–a woman Spring
thought she knew, a woman as beautiful
as Spring had ever seen; Persephone
put her hand out to Spring and forced a smile
as she moved toward Spring and black Hades.

> *I know now. Daddy came to my bed while Mommy
> was sleeping. He was the one who had kissed me
> saying everything is alright. Daddy pulled back my
> covers and got in my bed. He touched me and raped
> me every night. Until I built a wall. Stopped
> feeling. Stopped remembering. I must not tell. I
> must. I wish I could die.*

As she lay dying, Spring stretched out her hand
far into the ash, deep into her heart,
down into that black palace of hatred
where so long ago she had built a wall
to keep Persephone safe from her pain,
where she hoped Persephone waited now.
In the dark, the grey woman took her hand.

> *I remember now. All of it. I will not forget. I will
> not forgive. Nothing is alright. I am not fine. Will I
> ever be? Why did Mommy let this man take me?*

They touched hands and became as they had been;
Persephone entered and became Spring
as sunshine burst through the haze and flowers
blooming in the ash drove away the black
gyres that tormented Spring and held her down.
As Hades died a third and final time,
Spring took her first steps out of the darkness.

I still have the night terrors and daytime flashbacks. At least I understand now. Seeing my counsellor helps. And medications from my doctor. I don't talk to my mother. Did Persephone ever forgive Demeter? I wonder.

Susan

the lake 1973

I stand at the end of this long wood dock
looking across the lake's emerald calm
set among pine-furred mountain guardians
under a sky as blue as her eyes were once

behind me the hill curves upward softly
rolling rockface softened by shallow soil
spotted with scrub among soft wild grasses
to where my cabin backs up to the woods

at times in this silence I think of her
pale blue summer dress blowing in the breeze
here beside the lake smiling and waiting
fading away as early morning mist

legend says there's no bottom to this lake
where spirits rise with the first morning light
are seen by those who most need to see them
are felt near even when the mist has gone

from my cabin porch when the light is right
I almost see spectres rise through the mist
wavering forms that look almost human
but mostly I sense that Susan is near

between clear blue sky and emerald lake
these mountains are islands far from the world
where whispering winds may ease troubled minds
yet still I see Susan in waking dreams

the boys 1964

as a teen I set pins and clean washrooms
in the Chinook Centre's bowling alley
scour grills nights and weekends next door
at the sidewalk coffee shop in the mall

friends plan robberies they never commit
I don't build or explode bombs I design
in Kamph and Das Kapital are my texts
all in our afternoon coffee shop klatch

at the next table cats boast of luring
gay young barbers to bash in back alleys
ex-soldier brags he watched his colonel rape
a private then blackmailed him for silence

we young poets and painters test the line
never cross over to the other side
our game only to prove we could do it
I take my books back to the library

Susan 1969

walking down Eighth Avenue I see her
a woman I know from work or somewhere
hello Jimmy as she gets closer to me
and I say hello too and walk on by

I'd remember a woman this beautiful
walking into the bookstore where I work
buying a book or browsing the tables
but nothing tells me she was ever there

now I can't stop thinking of this woman
who greets me by my name then disappears
swallowed up by the busy downtown street
while I walk further along Eighth Avenue

city life 1968

the sun seems to whisper wake up Jimmy
I roll over to avoid the bright light
glad to be able to sleep until dawn
after six months in a northern work camp

it's a hard life working in the oil fields
grunt work from before dawn to after dusk
sleep in the bunk house with other young men
worth it when a man can be paid so well

back home in Calgary with six months' pay
I bought my new Mustang with oil field cash
the next week a blur of drinking and girls
got smart and got a job as cash ran out

once broke some juggers went back to the rigs
to bunk house blues and hard work in the fields
but I've managed to not blow all my wad
keep the Mustang and a job selling books

I started writing poems during oil field nights
stuck in the bunk house with not much to do
odd for a dropout who hated high school
the words just came and I wrote them all down

young poets came to the store and hung out
talked about readings in downtown cafés
asked me to come and read my own poems
my stories of the woods and of oil rigs

in cafés I read of heaven and hell
forests of pine and forests of derricks
my gateway to a new world of wonders
where the poets listen and accept me

Susan 1969

quiet talk washes over the café
hushes as I take my place on stage
begin reading to the usual crowd
then I remember her as she walks in

I stammer a bit as I read my set
carried away by eyes blue as the sky
wonder if a reading is where we'd met
look up just to see her walk out the door

like a ghost the woman is gone again
the woman who knows my name from somewhere
I should remember though I don't know why
she haunts me even when she is not here

the cabin 1972

I leave the highway onto the dirt track
into pine woods then turn in my driveway
park the car where it ends near the cabin
carry my load from that point to the dock

I feel at home in this lakeside cabin
bought in sixty-nine with oilfield savings
to escape the pressures of the city
be forgiven in the peace of the lake

my rowboat breaks the lake's placid surface
draws lines like fishbones along the water
to where I stop the boat at the center
do what I must then sit a while longer

once back at the dock I tie up the boat
watch the last of the sunrise over the lake
take a last look across the green water
drive back to town in a reverent mood

the chat 1969

like a James Stewart romantic movie
Susan and I meet by chance on the street
collide and all her parcels go flying
after apologies we trade names and talk

late in the fall I've finally met her
coffee and chat in a downtown café
all the usual getting to know you
Jimmy and Susan together at last

I still don't know where I've met her before
but suppose it doesn't really matter
Susan and I spend our best time together
days and evenings of life in the present

the here and now is good enough for me
the past will wait a time to let it out
set Susan free from what she fears the most
while now she's still a mystery to me

the fall 1971

she's still magic to me after four years
Susan of the soft blue eyes and deep soul
secrets in her past that she can't reveal
won't tell even to her longtime lover

even now Susan keeps her past to herself
between us a wall that I can't get past
at times I see terror too in her eyes
created by things she may see or hear

Susan still resists living together
keeps her apartment close as her secrets
looks over her shoulder far too often
nothing I can do from behind the wall

fear 1972

something happened as the new year began
terror overcame Susan's state of mind
as shadows of her past came to haunt her
where she hid behind a wall of secrets

fear seemed to build a newer higher wall
at last to shut me out almost completely
not able to free Susan from her past
not able to help her in the present

one argument too many over secrets
too many words said in haste and anger
Susan left my life quiet as she'd come
without fanfare or goodbye she was gone

it was as though she had never existed
the phone she never answered was cut off
rent never paid to hold her apartment
her work called the police with concern

the favour 1972

when Susan had asked me one last favour
I resisted though Susan's mind was set
to go ahead with or without my help
and I couldn't let her go it alone

Susan and I sat and talked all that night
until Susan slept while I held her hand
waiting for the first morning light to come
then took Susan with me to the cabin

the lake 1973

standing at the end of the dock at dawn
watching the sky in early light turn blue
my thoughts turn to city night images
the blue of Susan's eyes and her blonde hair

looking out over the lake just at dawn
I see Susan sometimes or think I do
the Lady of the Lake there in the mist
rising from the water then gone again

they say the lake is bottomless
they say a body in the lake will sink
but may float up if you wait long enough
ghost on the water then gone forever

snapshots from the attic

in grandpa's attic after he died
a mystery box filled with snapshots
facets of a life he must have known
never shared with family until now

a monk leans on the riverside rail
plays guitar at Chelsea Embankment
sings folk songs in a heavenly voice
like angels two crows circle above

someone has retouched this photograph
erased something from the dawning sky
birds perhaps or angels as they pass
parents and two kids look out in awe

a girl tunes her guitar in the bunkhouse
plays it tenderly as an old friend
her voice like a bell chimes off the cliffs
the lake holds the moon in its waters

a boy and girl walk on a dirt path
beside a forest-green mountain lake
behind them mom and dad hand in hand
loving words now frozen in the past

an old man sits in a rocking chair
a perfect view from the verandah
golden fields of his youth long ago
the old man's mind wanders into sleep

on the front steps a girl reads a book
her thoughts far off in a dark attic
with Anne Frank her own age lost to war
across the meadow a deer watches

a boy chases a dog through the grass
one sunny prairie day in the west
enjoying the warmth of summer sun
until dusk fades all to shades of grey

a woman stands alone on the verge
before her the deep blue lake water
touching the sky without horizon
until dusk covers the lake and her

the meal may be breakfast or dinner
three adults seated at the table
near the man a woman feeds the dog
the other watches the camera warily

this man clings at the end of a crane
tower below wrapped in fire and smoke
fingers of fire reach to caress him
rescue from a copter reels him in

an old man walks down a lonely street
into the waiting shadows of night
head bowed in sorrow he can't explain
even if someone would listen to him

a woman sits weeping on the shore
her sorrow unwarmed by the sunrise
in a world painted in shades of blue
where tears do not matter to a lake

a toddler wields a pink piece of chalk
draws a large pink cat on the sidewalk
cat energy expressed in slant lines
the essential cat sensed by a child

a boy runs on eternal green fields
sails his kite across a clean blue sky
away from the dark he knows is there
over and over into the sunshine

rockets explode and a city burns
not far away festive people cheer
watching the fireworks in the dusk
the eastern sun sits low in the sky

here a boy sits on a broken wall
waits for his mother without moving
the hospital destroyed by a bomb
at sunset she has not come for him

a dog walks beside a wooden fence
black shadow against early spring snow
moves with grace across this white silence
still the snow falls as soft as a cloud.

rowing from the dock near the cabin
the boy stops in the eye of the lake
that quiet place right at the centre
breeze blowing soft as mountain gods' breath

from the marsh along the wooded path
a frog chorus serenades lovers
in the open water two swans pause
greet these lovers walking hand in hand

a girl plays and sings songs in the dark
her face lit by the moon and the stars
fireflies flicker brightly around her
guitar strings echo sparks from the fire

a homeless child abandoned to the streets
peers from a dark space between buildings
the child shivers in the bitter wind
a man looks away and walks on past

this woman stands still as a statue
her self in the mirror worlds away
watches herself in the reflection
sees in the shadows an empty gown

a boy sits in a boat on the lake
blue as the clear mountain sky above
sapphire set in rich green pine forest
hears loons and ancient voices whisper

bent under his burden of sorrow
a soldier walks down a dusty road
nowhere to go to hide from the war
memories of death that he carries

these old men walk like Walter Brennan
carry canes like swords for self-defence
hunch around tables outside cafés
talk about times past without regret

this man and woman bask in the sun
in love with each other for all time
face the spring sunshine in defiance
live despite the end they know must come

two women meet at the edge of town
each in her Sunday best dress and hat
parasols set against the sunlight
talk away from prying eyes and ears

a woman in small-town Michigan
makes her home a shrine to her idol
statues and candles and his music
portraits of Elvis on black velvet

someone's grandmother rests on a beach
army truck ruts crisscross the gravel
an old woman alone as night falls
city lights fade across the water

an old man sits on a tattered couch
one bomb and war has taken the house
only rubble remains behind this couch
the end of his world as the sun sets

hope appears out of the battle's smoke
the flag she carries sags to the street
an old woman clings to the broken mast
shouts her anger to the empty street

a trapper sits beside his cabin
hides hung up to dry and firewood stacked
the dog waits quiet at the man's side
a peaceful moment as the day ends

a woman and man sit on a log
daughter behind them holding a cat
four men come out of the open door
the only sound is the powder's flash

night falls over the city of light
shadow people walk the downtown street
a large window reflects this darkness
shadows fade into the black of night

three blonde children sit on a brick fence
bathed in the pink glow as the sun sets
New York City sits on the far shore
the distant jewel fades with the light

old houses dot faraway hillsides
the stoney beach feels like a wasteland
young woman in swimsuit and jacket
her head tossed back for the camera

this woman hopes to appear sexy
sits with dress pulled up to reveal legs
bares her shoulder and smiles for the shot
arms across her torso and legs crossed

the young woman sits alone on sand
on a crowded beach nobody cares
who watches and waits for somebody
on some days a beach can be lonely

in fifty-five après swim at the lake
a girl of twelve vamps for a photo
in the background mom is unaware
turns away and looks toward the lake

this young beggar girl against a wall
her look defiant or come hither
barefoot anger in a tattered dress
is waiting to break out of the frame

the pretty young woman stands stiffly
caught between depression and wartime
less smile or frown than a puzzled look
a portrait of 1939

this young man in his cool sunglasses
loves his new '40 ragtop Chevy
loves this new woman he holds so tight
he smiles and takes pride in ownership

the couple on their verandah stairs
nineteen-sixties American Gothic
four kids stand iconic by the stairs
nobody looks at anyone else here

the old woman in nightgown and robe
stands on a skateboard on a dirt path
parasol raised like Mary Poppins
cheered on by her man who holds her hand

a beautiful young woman stands tall
men in battle-garb dance before her
zip-ties ready to restrain justice
in one woman they fear more than war

the man carries his son down the road
dangers left behind in the city
evening rain hides tears of regret
endless night is about to begin

this girl in red stands on the clay road
between deep ruts made by army trucks
rivers of water from the hard rain
her world made only of blood-red clay

at the shot's centre the girl is key
like her mom planned to shoot it that way
dad stands unsmiling beside the teen
kid brother frowns in front but she smiles

four young women naked but for towels
waists loosely wrapped after the sauna
a light flashes and startles the women
the cameraman unseen and gone

this woman's held out hand says it all
get that camera away from me
in her eyes anger at intrusion
she turns to the stairs up to the house

sometimes in photos we can see souls
there were those who feared the camera
this magic box which took men's images
would also spirit away their souls

Poet Profile

Bob MacKenzie has been greatly influenced by growing up in Alberta with artist parents and now finds inspiration for writing during daily walks through woods and along waterfronts in and around Kingston, Ontario. His keen eye for detail shows in his talent for outdoor photography. Bob's ability to draw a wide variety of people into conversation results in astute observations on human nature in his writing, and his love of music from diverse genres allows his poetry to sing and dance its way through our complex world.

Bob MacKenzie's poetry has been published across North America and as far away as Australia, Greece, India, and Italy in publications that include The Literary Review of Canada, The Dalhousie Review, Windsor Review, and The Criterion. He's published eighteen volumes of poetry and prose-fiction and his work's appeared in numerous anthologies.

Bob has received a number of awards for his writing including an Ontario Arts Council grant for literature, a Canada Council Grant for performance, and a Fellowship to attend the Summer Literary Seminars in Tbilisi, Georgia.

For eighteen years Bob's poetry was spoken and sung live with original music by the ensemble Poem de Terre, and the group released six albums.

9 788182 539471